T0065616

EURO EXIT

Euro Exit

Why (and How) To Get Rid of the Monetary Union

Jean-Jacques Rosa

Algora Publishing
New York

Library of Congress Cataloging-in-Publication Data —

Rosa, Jean Jacques.
 [Euro. English]
 Euro exit: why and how to get rid of the monetary union / Jean-Jacques Rosa.
    p. cm.
    ISBN 978-0-87586-912-4 (soft cover: alk. paper)—ISBN 978-0-87586-913-1 (hard cover: alk. paper)—ISBN 978-0-87586-914-8 (ebook) 1. Euro. 2. Euro area. 3. Money—European Union contries. 4. Monetary policy—European Union countries. 5. European Union countries—Economic policy. I. Title.
    HG925.R67213 2012
    332.4'94—dc23
                        2012002328

Front Cover: © Rob Chatterson/Corbis

Printed in the United States

TABLE OF CONTENTS

INTRODUCTION

> *"United we win, divided we lose. Union makes strength."*
> — Aesop

> *"People of the same trade seldom meet together, even for merriment and diversion, but the conversation ends in a conspiracy against the public, or in some contrivance to raise prices."* — Adam Smith, The Wealth of Nations

> *Populist. n. and adj. 1. "A supporter of the rights and power of the people as opposed to the elites." 2. See "democratic."*

Euro skeptics correctly identified all the problems that would ensue from applying a single currency to dissimilar economies; and they were right, across the board. As predicted, the single currency has proved to be a fiasco, damaging national economies and depriving them of an essential shock absorber to help them over the bumps of the "great recession". But being right is small comfort in the present crisis. In a democracy, more heed should have been paid to the "populists" who spoke out against the centralizing, and as such reactionary, Maastricht constitution. But the elite, both public and private, left and right, were too full of themselves; and, brought together by their shared monopoly on power, doggedly followed their own narrowest interests to the detriment of the general welfare and standard of living. Although finally forced to acknowledge that they have led our economies into a complete dead end, they still have not drawn any lesson from this, and, having learned nothing from experience, can think of nothing better than to recommend yet another — utopian — policy of centralization for the continent, even though that was what caused the looming disaster in the first place. [1]

---

1 On all these points see Laurent Cohen-Tanugi's revealing little book, *Quand l'Europe s'éveillera*, Grasset 2011. The author recognizes all the failures of the two decades of centralized monetary policy (1990–2010), then concludes that the policy only failed because there was not *enough* centralization. Therefore we need to go further in the same direction, much further. This reminds me of those Soviet ultraconservatives who defended empire and bureaucratic centralism right up until the final catastrophe. The main difference is that European centralists claim, in some surreal way, to be con-

The most significant political divide in this new century is no longer the traditional conflict between left and right, as they both, once in power, apply almost identical prescriptions. "Globalization requires it," they say. A more profound, although still poorly articulated, clash is beginning to emerge: between the populism of the great bulk of ordinary citizens (whose horizon is essentially national) and a coalition of elites, elites of the state as well as those of the large corporations, whose intended scope is cosmopolitan and global.

The proactive construction of a European identity, and particularly that of a single currency which has served as its spearhead in recent years, has brought into focus the emerging major divide between people who are concerned about their standard of living, on the one hand, and public treasuries, big banks, and big business on the other, who are set on defending to the bitter end their financial advantage in the international capital markets through a mixed cartel that confuses the public and private.

In this organizational battle, the oligarchic and technocratic elites initially took the lead in Europe, taking advantage of the public's natural indifference to the in-

structing the oxymoron of a "pacifist empire", a rival to the great powers of the United States and China, which is to be global in influence but, thanks to its moral force alone, immune from the need for armed defense.

tricacies of monetary policy. But their designs, far from embodying the avant-garde of modernity as they would have us believe, are actually left over from a world that is disappearing, the one that existed before the information and organization revolution. It is the world of empires, conglomerates and centralization, not that of the internet, individual initiatives and the secession of small nations. The attempt to centralize Europe thus stands in the way of the organizational evolution most likely to improve living standards, and it is in the monetary domain that this handicap is proving most obvious. That is why the multinational cartel of the euro will not last. The war of secession has already begun.

1. AN UNREASONABLE CHOICE

European governments have ensnared themselves in the very monetary net they have been stubbornly weaving for several decades, and which they thought would somehow miraculously capture the revenues needed to escape the harsh necessity of a structural adjustment of their balance sheets. A long time in the making, since the dissolution of the quasi-fixed exchange rate system of Bretton Woods in 1971–73, and then again even more ambitiously after the failure of its substitutes, the "snake" of European currencies followed by the European monetary system (EMS), the abolition of national currencies and their replacement by a shared currency — the euro — has turned against its proponents in the turbulence of 2007–2009.

This should come as no surprise. Monetary integration of quite dissimilar economies, obstinately carried out
in defiance of all economic analysis, was a fundamental error whose failure could be predicted by theory alone, even
before the creation of the euro.[2] It was foreseeable, and
the error was indeed predicted by experts, at least those
who were independent enough to think outside the "politically correct" box. And it is unfolding today in exact
accordance with the teachings of modern macroeconomic
theory.

By definition, the creation of a single currency implied
the loss of domestic national monetary policies — interest rates and exchange rates — that are essential tools for

---

2 "The creation of the single currency, the euro, is the most serious economic error committed by European governments
   since the deflationary policies that transformed the stock
   market crisis of 1929 into a decade of global depression
   throughout the 1930s. It leads to an even more serious political error: the attempt to merge the nation states of the
   continent into a single state very large." That's what I wrote
   in 1998 on the eve of the launch of the euro, at the conclusion
   of my book *Euro Error* (French original by Grasset, English
   edition Algora 1999).
Earlier, in 1991, the most thorough and most consistent of "euro
   skeptics" Martin Feldstein, president of the prestigious
   National Bureau of Economic Research, perfectly forecast
   the future negative economic consequences and the political conflicts that the euro would create, in a variety of
   communications, including a resounding article, "Europe's
   Monetary Union: The Case Against EMU," published by *The
   Economist*, June 13, 1992.

---

cushioning the effects of the inevitable shocks and fluctuations in economic conditions. These have been replaced by a centralized monetary policy that is incapable of meeting the needs of any of the member countries, whose circumstances usually differ and which have continued to do so since the inception of the euro: one size fits none. At the first major crisis, reasonably competent and professionally independent economists[3] warned, the national economies' divergences would become acute, would require corrective monetary policies specific to each country, and thus would lead to an abandonment of the centralized policy. That is precisely where we are now, in the tidal bore of the "great recession", the worst one that we have experienced since the 1930s.

Held up as a panacea in official speeches, the euro has become a problem in reality, and even those who only yesterday were swearing by it, in spite of all realities, are now wondering how best to "save" it even while they really fear that it is already dead.[4]

---

3 For example individuals as diverse in their theoretical approaches as Paul Krugman and Martin Feldstein, joined later by Milton Friedman, and more recently by Joseph Stiglitz.
4 Since the beginning of the international financial crisis, more and more commentators have concluded, as Charles Calomiris recently wrote, that "The Euro Is Dead" (*Foreign*

But the same causes produce the same effects. Bail-outs, aid to insolvent states, and other attempts at fiscal policy coordination, will not help: it is the very system of the euro that is at question, and this system is inherently self-destructive.

The bright side is that, as the euro is fundamentally pathogenic to the continent's economies, its termination should not be feared but welcomed instead, as an opportunity for future growth. It's a matter of elementary logic: if the euro exerts globally harmful effects on the economy, which is widely recognized today after ten years of experience, the removal of this burden can only be beneficial and wealth increasing.[5]

But when the dissolution of the euro is followed by a recovery of economic growth, the ruling elites in politics, administration and business who have been so bent on creating the euro[6] might have to admit the ineptitude

Policy, January 6, 2011). However, Calomiris proposes, in an original but illogical way, to resurrect it later.

5 In fact, the magnitude of the growth that has been missed during the euro years (and during the 1990s due to policies aimed at preparing for monetary union by converging toward the Maastricht criteria) means we can actually envisage a good few years of prosperity in a catching-up process after the euro goes away, just as European economies did during the *"trente glorieuses,"* the thirty high growth post-War years.

6 For a list of some of them, take a look at who signed the manifesto published in *Le Monde*, October 28, 1997, excerpts of

of their centralist creed and the immense responsibility that rests on their shoulders for progressively stifling the growth of our economies for nearly a quarter century.[7] It is therefore not surprising that these leaders use every imaginable expedient (all of them costly), not to save the single currency that continues to hamper the economic activity of member countries (saving the single currency is basically an impossible task) but to defer for as long as possible the moment of truth that will result in a return to national currencies. As these expedients are many and their uses vary from one country to another, it follows that the actual course and timeframe for the dissolution of the euro cannot be precisely forecast. But the direction of change can hardly be doubted. Euro skeptics have won the intellectual battle hands down.

Economists are pretty broadly in agreement now, although this realization came late in France and Europe, recognizing the impossibility of maintaining a single currency in 17 countries having different structures and circumstances (in other words, in a non-optimal currency area, a "non-OCA") without a budgetary union. And a

which appear in Appendix II.

7 Including the years leading up to and preparing for approval of the euro, during which the policies of convergence that were applied by the candidate countries prefigured what would ultimately be the policy of the single currency, with all its negative consequences.

sustainable budgetary union can only be achieved by a central government, or in other words a federal state. This conclusion was clear to few observers in Europe ten or twenty years ago,[8] just a small minority. But the political and fiscal centralization, that many hope is still possible, faces fundamental and currently insurmountable obstacles which can be explained through economic analysis.[9] It is this organizational impossibility of budgetary integration that entirely rules out a monetary union in a non-optimal currency area, and at the same time makes such efforts harmful and unreasonable.

But if this is the case, we must explain the extraordinary obstinacy of the Unionists. One sign suggests the underlying reasons why they stick to their guns so unreasonably, and that is the extreme hyperbole they employ

---

8 In France, in particular, the number of economists who criticized the euro could be counted on the fingers of one hand, or two hands at the very most. Just four were consistently opposed: Alain Cotta, Gérard Lafay, Jean-Pierre Vespérini, and this author. Some others took more or less guarded positions, depending on their circumstances and their professional obligations.

9 This analysis of the disintegration of large hierarchical structures during periods of growing information abundance (such as the current IT revolution) is the theme of my book *Le second vingtième siècle : déclin des hiérarchies et avenir des nations* [*The Second Twentieth Century : Decline of Hierarchies and the Future of Nations*] (Grasset 2000, and Hoover Press 2006 for the English edition).

when talking up the euro. Why, one may ask, did they feel compelled to attribute to the use of a single currency such unlikely virtues as representing a "shield against financial and economic crises", providing an "acceleration of growth through a strong currency," or a way to make national business conditions and inflation rates converge, or to eliminate resistance to liberalization and reform, while improving budget equilibriums, all assertions that were quickly put to the test in reality and shown to be false[10]? Isn't it that they knew they needed to quell the widespread doubts the Euro skeptics had spread in public opinion, by "over acting," as in bad theater? In bad theater, actors play in an exaggerated way because the script is weak. With the euro, the putative benefits had to be exaggerated because they were actually non-existent, while the disadvantages were severe and very real. However, if the virtues of the euro were much less than its promoters claimed, they must have been looking for some other outcome than improving the standard of living of the general public. But, in this case, what exactly?

It is this missing explanation that we propose to uncover in the following pages, and then we will turn to a consideration of the possible ways out of the quagmire

---

10 See my 2002 article: "Les promesses de l'euro : tout était faux" ("The Promises of the Euro : They Were All False"), available at http://jeanjacques.rosa.pagesperso-orange.fr

into which the euro has sunk our economies — and of those paths that appear to be closed. First of all, we must recall the reasons why the euro is not viable.

Replacing the national currencies with the euro was an unreasonable decision in economic terms. In fact, it could only lead to a slow-down in the growth of living standards in Europe. The reason is simple: monetary policy is a major instrument by which governments can influence economic activity, stimulating it when there are shocks that slow growth, and push towards recession, or conversely moderating growth when the economy is overheating and there is a danger of increased inflation. Monetary policy basically consist of adjusting the interest rates set by the central bank, which simultaneously affects the amount of credit supplied by banks (and the demand for it by households and businesses) as well as capital inflows or outflows that affect the exchange rate with other currencies. The exchange rate, in turn, affects exports and imports by changing the price of national goods abroad and the prices of foreign goods in the domestic market.

In an open economy, the exchange rate is by far the most important of all prices. Indeed, it affects the prices of all exports and all imported goods at the same time, and thus impacts very directly the activities of every firm operating in the country that either exports or produces goods and services that compete with imports. The abolition of exchange rates with certain trading partners is thus fraught with consequences.

The results are even worse when the monetary union is not "optimal", and its effects cannot be offset by other economic policies (federal fiscal transfers, for instance) and when political integration is impossible under existing conditions.

Immiserizing Monetary Unions

In the early 1960s, Robert Mundell, Ronald McKinnon and Peter Kenen developed the theory of "optimum currency areas."[11] It traces the conditions under which many countries might benefit from sharing a single currency (and thus a single monetary policy) in place of the several currencies in existence. The idea is simple. Money is the basis of monetary policy and monetary policy is useful in stabilizing the economy. It increases the average growth rate because, when adequately used, it can reduce the severity of recessions. Thus, a single currency will be beneficial when various national economies are in sync,

11 An economist colleague of mine, a fierce partisan of the euro, seeing how astonished I was that this theory was totally neglected during debates on the passage of the euro in France in the 1990s, gave the surprising response, "but this is an old theory!", as if one could tell whether an analysis was true or not just by knowing what was the latest theoretical fashion.

that is, when they experience similar dynamics, both in terms of real activity and in terms of inflation. A single monetary policy is, in this case, well suited to the economic circumstances of each of the nations involved, as they are all in phase at any given time.

It is important that the inflation rates be similar, because different rates of inflation lead to loss of export competitiveness for the country where costs are increasing the most. And the most convenient instrument for restoring competitiveness then is a depreciation of the currency, which reduces the price of exports sold abroad and thus compensates for the higher domestic inflation, without the need to reduce domestic prices through deflation (which is always undesirable because it entails an economic slowdown and increased unemployment). Thus, economies in which inflation rates are usually in sync with each other are not harmed by moving to a single currency regime. But it is essential that their inflation rates evolve similarly.

If, and only if, this is the case, a shared currency is superior to independent currencies circulating in smaller areas, as a single currency lowers transaction costs in international trade. When the economies are in sync and labor is mobile, the problems caused by a single currency are limited and the advantages in terms of increased ease of transactions predominate. The currency area is then "optimal" and it benefits the economy.[12]

A single currency is still acceptable, even for economies that are not in sync cyclically, if the factors of production are mobile between regions and countries. It is also a preferred solution for a small country trading mostly with a larger neighbor, which is its main customer and main supplier. Adopting the currency of that neighbor removes the risk of massive exchange rate shocks that would destabilize the smaller economy, which has no choice but to remain very open and very dependent on foreign trade — and all the more so when this trade represents a large share of GDP and is geographically concentrated.

However, reviewing the characteristics of European countries that joined the euro zone, it is easy to see that they do not belong to an optimal currency area. Indeed, their economies are not synchronized; their inflation rates are different and are diverging; and the international mobility of labor is very limited: the unemployed of Naples rarely look for work in Madrid, Strasbourg or Berlin. Small countries like Luxembourg, the Netherlands, and even Austria, with close commercial ties to Germany and with

---

12 The savings to be found in reduced transaction costs resulting from monetary union are of little practical consequence. Official reports have estimated it at a few tenths of one percent of the zone's GDP.

similar inflation rates, could be part of a Deutsche-mark optimal zone. But France, Italy, Spain and Ireland are not part of a common optimal currency area, whether the mark zone or the euro zone.

Under these circumstances, removing the option of using national monetary policies significantly reduces the effectiveness of economic stabilization policy, and thus also reduces growth in the long run, in the absence of another appropriate instrument to cushion them from recessions. A single monetary policy cannot suit all countries simultaneously. And so the single currency reduces income (relative to what it would be with an adequate national monetary policy) in those countries that adopt it.

To counter this observation, one may hold up the hope that these national economies may converge in the future and eventually become more homogeneous, simply due to the monetary unification and the development of trade it is supposed to promote. This assumption, however, was rejected on theoretical grounds by Paul Krugman, Nobel laureate and a specialist in economic geography, who showed that increased trade does not lead to the homogenization of economic activities within a given territory, but on the contrary to more national or regional specialization. Even today in the U.S., where the currency union is of long standing, a strong regional specialization of activities can be observed: information technology in California, automobiles in Detroit, the oil industry in Texas, and so on. These different industries are not experiencing synchronous business cycles, and thus the various states are not, either. We must not expect either a convergence of economic cycles within the euro zone; and neither have we seen one, after ten years of experience in Europe. Spain is not in sync with Germany, nor Germany with Ireland, and the differences in inflation rates are increasing over time.[13]

Even so, proponents of the euro use the example of the monetary union in the United States as yet another argument in their favor.

Non-Optimal Monetary Areas, Viable and Non Viable

Various studies have shown that different regions of the United States (the Northeast, the South, California,

---

13 The notion that economies will automatically converge as a sole result of adopting one currency is inherently absurd. Taken to the extreme, it implies that if every country in the world were to adopt the same form of money (gold, for example), their real economies would all come to resemble one another and the whole planet would be transformed into one optimal currency area. Any collection of nations could thus become an optimal currency area just by choosing their currency. That is like saying that currency is all powerful in determining the development and structure of real economies.

the Midwest, etc.) do not meet the criteria for a common optimal currency area, in part because of the different specializations mentioned above, and in spite of the fact that the mobility of labor is incomparably higher between American states than between European states. Hence the argument of the Unionists: if the U.S. is not an optimal currency area, but nevertheless has been a single currency area, and for a long time, why can't Europe do the same?

They forget that there is a major difference, which is political. The United States has long been a federal state that collects high taxes as a share of GDP. This enables the US to make automatic compensatory redistribution among member states when things get out of whack. If Texas is growing while Michigan is in a recession, federal tax revenues will be abundant in Texas and can be used to assist the unemployed in Michigan. While monetary policy cannot correct these imbalances among states, as the same monetary policy prevails in all of them, federal fiscal policy can.

That's why nobody seriously envisages a future when "regional dollars" would replace the current U.S. dollar under the pretext of implementing a regional monetary policy that could be more effective than the Federal monetary policy, which by definition is unique. The United States is not an optimal currency area, actually, but the disadvantages are outweighed by the existence of a fed-eral fiscal policy. This non-optimal currency area is thus made "practicable", or viable, by the budgetary union.

But for such transfers to be made between indepen-dent countries, there has to be a legitimate political au-thority capable of collecting taxes from the taxpayers of some countries in order to help, sometimes massively, citizens of other nations. This does not exist in Europe, where the union's taxes are quite low compared to na-tional taxes and are used primarily for agricultural subsi-dies under CAP (The Common Agricultural Policy). And the reluctance of countries from Northern Europe to pay for aid to Greece currently illustrates all the difficulties of such transfers when there is no federal political union; it also raises the question of whether such a unification is even possible, if the people in question do not feel a suf-ficient degree of common solidarity.

Moreover, political centralization appears to be im-possible in the advanced information society of the late twentieth and early twenty-first century.

Harmful Federalism

To offset the negative effects of being a non-optimal currency area, and in order to make it "practicable", a central political authority would be required. But then the same question arises as to the shared currency: under what conditions is a central state better for the people concerned than the several states that currently exist?

The standard answer is similar whether the question is about the currency or the state, and it has to do with having relatively homogeneous populations. Indeed, a state produces goods and "public" services which are basically available in the same quantity for all users. As such, national defense is a service that is provided in just about the same way for all residents of a country, as are the law and the legal system.

Populations that have very different preferences regarding national defense and legal systems obviously have an interest in separating from each other and creating their own distinct states that can produce these public goods at the specific level that suits them. We saw, for example in the Gulf Wars, that various European countries opted for different forms of political intervention or no intervention at all. In this case being obliged to subscribe to one single foreign policy has angered many of the national populations, which means it has lowered their level of satisfaction, which is a factor to be considered when calculating the actual standard of living.

In other words, these European countries are not part of an "optimal state area," a term that I proposed as a counterpart to that of optimum currency area in my book *Euro Error*.

Never mind, reply the Federalists, we have to have a federal state anyway, since on the one hand this will give us the power we need in an uncertain globalized world, and on the other hand it will end up forcing European citizens toward a convergence of preferences that will justify the initial creation of the state, after the fact.

Such a construction is highly unlikely today, however, as I show in my book *Le second vingtième siècle, déclin des hiérarchies et avenir des nations* (The Second Twentieth Century: Decline of Hierarchies and Future of Nations), which extends the discussion on "optimal state areas" started in *Euro Error*. The construction of such a super-state (in other words, a state that is superimposed on the existing national states) has no chance of success under the conditions of the late twentieth and early twenty-first centuries. The reason is organizational.

For such political integration to be beneficial (given the heterogeneity of the populations) the administration of the very large state (a population of over 320 million administered in the euro area, or nearly 500 million in the 27 countries of the EU) would have to be more efficient than that of a smaller state (comprising say 40, 50, or 60 million citizens). All these states operate on the hierarchical principle: they are large bureaucratic conglomerates of bureaucracies.[14] This is also true of firms, but generally on a smaller scale. The development and size of these hierarchies ultimately depends on their efficiency compared with that of decentralized mechanisms, relying on external market exchanges. As big hierarchies are replaced by smaller ones the extent of markets in production grows and the overall organization of society evolves towards decentralization. A decentralized organization of production requires more information than a centralized one. By the same token, large hierarchies use information relatively sparingly, while small hierarchies and the more developed markets rely on large amounts of information by unit of production.[15]

Of course, since the last quarter of the twentieth century (1975 marks a turning point in several dimensions) we have been living in an age of information revolution, seeing the complete reinvention of information technology and communications (computers, internet). The decentralization of all organizations, both public and private, has been possible as a result of these changes. This has led to a general reduction in the average size of hi-

14 These bureaucracies are all organized according to the nested or "Russian *matryoshka* doll" organizational structure.
15 This point is further developed in my book *Le second vingtième siècle.*

erarchies (in firms as well as states) and accelerated the development of global markets, or in other words "globalization." The rise of global markets in itself eliminates the need for large domestic markets: Swiss and Swedish industries, which can export around the world, are just as competitive as U.S. industries that benefit from a large internal market. It follows that the large nation states no longer have an economic advantage over smaller ones, as they had back when the global economy was fragmented and trade was obstructed by protectionism and the high cost of transport and communications. Under these new conditions, smaller nations such as Canada, Sweden and New Zealand can prosper, and the advantage of very great nations or empires is reduced to a trickle. The growing number of relatively small nations, and the end of the Bretton Woods fixed exchange rate system, are part of that evolution, as are secessionist and regionalist movements.

The era of federal states and empires was the late nineteenth and early twentieth century. The advantage now lies with small states, even the smallest of them. This transformation is the exact opposite of that which marked the end of the nineteenth century, during the second industrial revolution that brought forth the emergence of giant corporations and the establishment of the great modern empires: such was the case of the United

States after the Civil War, the German Reich with the war against Austria and then against France, the unification of Italy after a brief revolution, and Japanese expansionism through imperialist aggression.

Today, however, we have just witnessed the disintegration of empires, and since 1991 only one survives, though the very term empire might be challenged in the case of the current dominant power, the United States.

In this context the idea of creating a centralized political authority of broad scope in Europe is, to say the least, improbable, if not impossible. The theme has also been dropped in official communications. The recantations of the Lisbon Treaty, as well as failures in what few popular consultations have been held on the issue of the "Constitutional" Treaty (in Ireland and in France) show that current developments are pointing in the opposite direction. The failures of the euro only drive the point home.

The rescue funds set up recently to help Greece, and soon Portugal and Spain, cannot really be counted as the beginning of any true solidarity between nations within the zone. They are not actually intended to restore the economies of these countries, nor the prosperity of their citizens; they are further increasing these countries' debt. The loans are tied to compulsory austerity policies that exacerbate the recession, ultimately causing an increase of the ratio of debt to GDP by the contraction of the national product. This "aid" leads to the trap of debt deflation for the economies they are supposed to save. In fact, their main purpose is to stave off the bankruptcy of large banks, especially German and French banks, who have been feasting on the debts of those states — debts that are euro-denominated and thus in principle guaranteed against currency depreciation; debts that are particularly profitable since they get refinanced at low cost by the ECB. This is essentially a form of national aid for domestic banks.

The prospects of creating a federal state like the United States, the German Reich and Italy, all of which were created in the nineteenth century, and all through war, whether civil or foreign, are now nonexistent for reasons relating to the conditions underlying the evolution of organizational structures in an era of rapid progress in information and communication technologies (ICT).

The most likely conclusion as to the future of the single currency is, therefore, that there will be no federal shock absorber to coordinate fiscal transfers between nations, taking the place of the domestic shock absorbers that the independent currencies and flexible exchange rates represented. The national economic machineries inside the zone are now at the mercy of every shock that may arise, and they will be hit hard.

But even worse, on top of all that, we have to add the fact that the single currency encourages destabilizing economic behaviors that amplify expansions as well as recessions, a mechanism that is inherently destabilizing.

An Inherently Destabilizing Mechanism

So the euro zone is not an optimal currency area; it is not a non-optimal currency area that could be made "feasible" by creating a federal state to manage transfers to compensate for differences in economic circumstances, and it is out of the question that it can be turned into one since it is not an "optimal *state* area." But in addition, the way national inflation rates diverge even while operating in the context of a single currency creates perverse incentives that exacerbate economic imbalances across the board. The Central Bank in Frankfurt effectively sets a single interest rate for all member states. That means that countries with relatively low inflation compared to the ECB's nominal rate, which are probably countries where economic activity is weak, will end up with higher real interest rates (inflation-adjusted). In fact, the lower their own inflation is, the higher the real interest rate will be. And an economy in recession will be confronted with even higher real interest rates, and the deeper the recession, the worse the real rates will be. And if the country's economy slips into deflation, the ECB rate will further delay its recovery.

By contrast a booming economy will experience higher inflation, which will reduce its real interest rates by a similar amount, making the economy even more likely to overheat. Inflation then goes up a little more, further reducing real interest rates and promoting all sorts of speculation on assets whose supply is inelastic, such as land and property assets. This results in speculative "bubbles" which are designed to explode at the slightest economic hitch, including inflation or an increase in the ECB's interest rates.

The single monetary policy puts the brakes on economies that are already in recession and stimulates those that are overheating. It cannot help but be profoundly destabilizing, contrary to the original claim that it would be a "shield" against economic and financial crises.

Banks in the euro area thus faced huge temptations to develop massive, increasingly dubious loans the return of which is pumped up by the real estate price bubble, and through easy ECB refinancing thanks to the euro. Investors were encouraged to borrow more because of falling real interest rates (due to rising prices), and the banks wanted to lend more because their real rate of refinancing also fell, for the same reason: the ECB was refinancing them at a constant nominal rate independent of local inflation. This mechanism in turn fed the surge in housing prices, notably in Ireland and Spain, which in turn reduced the real interest cost of these financial operations.

Against the background of this speculative over borrowing, certain euro-zone member states found themselves facing a major recession (2007–2009) which they could not fight by adjusting exchange rates. (Instead, the euro was revalued massively against the dollar and vis-à-vis the economies tied to the dollar.) They have seen their economies tumble. In these circumstances, what could governments do? They were denied the right to follow an appropriate monetary policy. The only weapon they had left was to run budget deficits — which is even more tempting when the cost of borrowing is reduced by both the guarantee of the capital, based on the strong euro, and the actual real interest rates reduced by inflation. The governments of the most vulnerable economies, whether they depend on tourism and lax fiscal management (as in Greece) or were hit by the bursting housing bubbles (Ireland and Spain), had to turn to the only stabilizing tool they still had — budget deficits. Deficits that pushed them to the brink of insolvency. In these circumstances an independent currency would have plunged in value, limiting their ability to borrow in foreign currency and therefore limiting the accumulation of debt. But the strong euro made it possible to extend sovereign debt much further. And this was the end of its alleged virtue of enhancing fiscal soundness.

Thus, clearly, the economic case for the euro was very poor, even disastrous, even before it was implemented. This has been more than confirmed, in all respects, by later events. Yet those economists who expounded such arguments have not been heard. Rather, they have been excluded from public debate in favor of the mainstream professionals who obediently toed the line, praising with the politicians, government officials and business leaders the extraordinary benefits that the single currency was supposed to bring to European economies.

On the rare occasions when a serious debate did take place, pro-euro economists painted themselves into a corner. As a last resort they fell back on the argument of authority: "There may be some economic disadvantages to the euro, but the reasons for its creation were not economic but political." They were echoing Martin Feldstein's conclusion: the euro would have to bring sound political benefits to offset all its economic drawbacks.[16]

The question that naturally arises is, what political benefits are substantial enough to offset the economic losses that the euro inevitably imposes on the participating economies?

---

16 "The Political Economy of the European Economic and Monetary Union: Political Sources of an Economic Liability", *Journal of Economic Perspectives* Volume 11, Number 4. Fall 1997, pp. 23-42.

2. But What Political Advantage?

To understand that, we must look again at the economic nature of the euro in order to grasp what its political utility might be. The fact that the goals of monetary union are "political" is not in itself sufficient justification for the union. We would also need to clarify what is meant by "political," how this might offer advantages worth the sacrifices entailed, and for whom.

The adjective "political" actually covers several different meanings and here we use mainly three, corresponding to as many motivations guiding collective choices in different polities. These can be defined as follows:

    (A) The pursuit of the interests of the population as a whole, that is to say, mainly, improving average living standards through the provision of public goods by a benevolent social planner. This is presumed to occur in a democracy where the leaders are effectively subject to voter preferences.

(B) The mere will to power of the ruling elites, or "hubris," in a system where the leaders are independent of the voters, which is a "managerial" political system — as is the case in businesses where the manager pursues his own interest instead of serving the shareholders' interests.

(C) The pursuit of particular interests by pressure groups that exert a decisive influence on political leaders, in a regime where those "factions" that Madison feared, are particularly powerful. This would be the case in an oligarchy or a technocracy.

The economic analysis presented above shows the negative effects the euro would have on living standards, and the fact that Europe is not an "optimal state area," lead us to discard the first proposition concerning any "political" advantages of the euro. The euro is not a "public good" that might improve the welfare of the general population. It is more like a "public bad" that can only pull down the standard of living, or at least be a drag on growth.

The second meaning asserts the goal of a "Europe as a great power". This means forcing the Europeans to go ahead and build a super-state, which they are reluctant to do, by the artificial technique of a monetary union, which sooner or later will force them to accept a fiscal union just as well, and therefore a federal state. That new super state would be the second or maybe even the first world power, which could hardly displease the political and administrative class of its member countries.[17]

But it is reasonable to ask how that justifies the business leaders' enthusiasm for the euro. Political power is not a priority for them that outweighs the promotion of their own business interests. Indeed, business people rarely show high political ambition, especially if it is going to shrink profits. Nevertheless the euro has been supported throughout by a coalition of political leaders, administrative elites, and leaders of big business.[18] So there must be other motives and other interests at stake.

It follows that we have to turn, by default, to the third hypothesis, that of motivation corresponding to particular interests, interests that are shared by certain "factions" or pressure groups which have nothing to do with the

---

17 This is the option that Christian Saint-Etienne approves with lyrical emphasis in his book, *La puissance ou la mort.* For him, the "end of the euro," which he mentions in a more recent work, is something we must avoid at all costs, and the nations of Europe must give all the concerted effort necessary to save it and prevent its collapse. Obviously, such propositions are received very warmly in official circles where they justify and bolster the conventional opinion.

18 See Appendix II, below.

public interest nor indeed with any ambition to have a decisive influence in world affairs.

What might these interests be? The fact that they unite in a single coalition politicians of every stripe, government officials, and business leaders, gives us a lead. Those interests must be common to the state apparatus, as an organization defending its own survival and its own expansion, on the one hand (for politicians and civil servants), and to big business on the other (for corporations). What then do they have in common?

The statutory definition of the euro provides the explanation: The new currency, according to the agreements governing its creation, must be unique and strong. We must therefore look at how these two features might objectively benefit those groups who argue in its favor. Economically, the answer is pretty simple: the major borrowers — debt issuers — directly benefit from a strong single currency, because debt expressed in such a currency is very much in demand by investors worldwide as the redemption value is secure and because the large European market provides greater liquidity than smaller national ones. Investors therefore require relatively low interest rates, a boon for the borrowers whose cost of capital is thus reduced.

And we know who the major borrowers are: the states, the "new" banks that reinvented their business in the 1980s, and big businesses. They all need to attract large amounts of the new international capital that is being traded on the global financial markets since the last quarter of the twentieth century.

But the single currency has yet another advantage: It makes it easier to manage the intra-European price agreements that producer cartels are so fond of. The completion of the common market (in 1986 with the "single act"), was a strong incentive for these cartels to reorganized themselves from the national to the continental level. For the producer cartels, multiple currencies were a puzzle that made price agreements difficult to enforce. With a single currency, these price agreements become transparent and can be managed far more effectively than through multiple currencies linked by fluctuating exchange rates. The single currency is a boon for cartels.

CARTELS AND DEBTORS' INTEREST

The benefits of a strong currency are thus easy to understand: it reduces domestic inflation and provides guarantees as to the value of future repayments of capital to international lenders. It promotes the inflow of international savings that are now abundantly available in a globalized world where capital movements have been freed. As a result, it reduces the premium that otherwise raises lending rates to offset the risk of inflation. When a strong currency policy is sustainable, the risk of future inflation fades and inflation premiums disappear. Permanent (or "structural") borrowers such as states and large firms benefit from this. With a strong currency, they get money cheaper, and, while the reduction in interest rates may seem small,[19] given the enormous volume of their borrowings, it is actually of great importance for their balance sheets and financing capacity.

On the other hand, obviously, a strong currency hinders exports. But for big corporations, globalized direct investment abroad has more and more taken the place of simply exporting goods and services, and a strong , currency means that it costs less to buy plants or firms overseas. In addition, a strong currency reduces the cost of importing intermediate products used in the production of finished goods. This is especially true of the "German model," where components are imported that have already been processed in Central and Eastern Europe in

---

19 Bond prices evolve inversely with market interest rates. For a fixed nominal coupon rate, a high demand for bonds reduces the market interest rate, and thus the cost of capital for borrowers' new public offerings — and a reduction of the expected inflation and devaluation risk premiums boosts the demand for bonds.

particular, which are then integrated into the Germanic products before re-export, whether to third countries or to other countries of the euro zone.[20] Examples include automobile engines manufactured in Hungary, Romania and Poland, which are then assembled with other car elements in Germany, and the sedans are subsequently exported to France, Italy, China or Africa. The countries of origin of these imports are not the same as the destination country of the final products, and given the differences in exchange rates, a profit can be made. The strong euro reduces the cost of imports from Eastern Europe while Germany's inflation rate, which is lower than that of France, Italy or Spain, promotes the export of finished products to these countries within the euro area.

But these effects of a strong currency are not sufficient to explain why the euro is so attractive to large firms and state treasuries. Indeed, a country with an independent currency can perfectly well manage it conservatively and take advantage of its strength in foreign exchange markets. That is what Germany did, for example, with the Deutsche mark, and what Switzerland is doing now. But fusing national currencies into one presents an additional advantage: the exchange rate becomes "permanently

---

20 On this point, see Hans-Werner Sinn, *Can Germany Be Saved*, MIT Press, 2007.

fixed", thus removing any foreign exchange risk within the zone and therefore eliminating the risk premiums that are inevitable in any floating exchange rate regime (as well as in fixed adjustable exchange rate regimes). Removing these risk premiums helps to lower lending rates.

Moreover, a single currency shared by several countries presents another type of benefit, and quite a significant one, at that. It makes it easier to compare domestic prices across the various member countries. Advocates of the euro have alleged that this benefits consumers, who otherwise were unable to accurately compare the price of a Volkswagen in Bonn, expressed in marks, with one in Paris, listed in francs, when the franc–mark exchange rate varied from day to day. In this environment, it is easy for companies to charge discriminatory rates because the lack of adequate consumer information.

This argument is misleading. Car buyers do not go and get a car in Bonn rather than in Paris anyway, not because they are unable to compare prices in these two cities but because other costs, including administrative fees (in France the "Mines" regulations on imports), more than outweigh any gains to be anticipated. Buyers shop where they are, as it is more economical and more convenient.

On the other hand, flexible exchange rates create difficulties for businesses that operate in several markets by impeding their anti competitive agreements, widespread in many industries. Oligopolistic structures are commonly found in most national economies in Europe.[21] The development of the common market, completed in 1986 with the "Acte unique européen", undermined the national oligopolies which were organized into cartels in order to reduce competition. The resulting increase of competition eroded their rents. Their next step, logically, was to seek to reconstruct the cartels, but this time on a Europe-wide scale in order to include their main competitors in a broader cartel. This task was undertaken by professional organizations lobbying in Brussels. However, they encountered one major difficulty: the operation of any cartel is based on restricting the volume of production, which can generate super profits in a quasi-monopoly way. But in order to work, they need not only limit the quantities of output but also enforce the agreed collusion price. The best known example is the organization that governs the oil-producing countries (OPEC). The price of oil is set

---

21 See for example the French Competition Authority's recent conviction of the French banks for cartel behavior (*Le Monde*, September 21, 2010). See also the general discussion by Nobel Prize-winner Edmund Phelps, « La contre-performance de l'Europe continentale : le lien entre institutions, dynamisme et prospérité économique», *Revue de l'OFCE*, January 2005, pp. 1-31, especially the passage on economic corporatism in Europe.

globally. But it is set in dollar terms, which makes it possible to monitor each member country's compliance with this *unique* price that is essential for the proper operation of any cartel. Monitoring is essential because each cartel member is strongly tempted to secretly give a slight discount to its customers. If it can do that, it becomes very competitive and beats the other producers that comply with the high price set by the cartel. By cheating just a little, it can increase sales ... and profits. But as this cheating becomes widespread, the cheating eventually blows the cartel agreement to pieces by leading to an increased supply and lower prices that eat up the super profits.

Therefore the life of a cartel is fragile and requires the close monitoring of producer prices. Prices have to be readily transparent to all, so that sanctions can be weighed against anyone who is cheating within the cartel. That is no easy task in an international cartel when exchange rates fluctuate daily. It is hard to determine what is the appropriate cartel price when changes in exchange rates would ordinarily justify a different price in each country. This requires a constant renegotiation of the cartel price — in each currency — a renegotiation that is difficult and costly.

Everything becomes easier for the cartels when prices are established in a single currency, without any change in exchange rates.

It follows that the reinvention of domestic cartels on a larger scale, in the common market, requires that national currencies be replaced by a single currency. Not for the benefit of consumers, but for the profits of producers.

All of these effects explain why big business has been so persistent in seeking to achieve the implementation of the single currency, after the failure of the "currency snake" and the "European monetary system" that earlier had attempted to reduce the market uncertainties. Both exchange rates agreements attempted to limit the range of exchange rates fluctuations between European countries, but failed precisely because these countries do not form a natural OCA. Accordingly, major shocks such as the oil shocks of the 1970s or the German reunification shock of the early 1990s made national real activities and inflation rates diverge, and as a consequence the nominal exchange rates also diverged beyond the authorized range of fluctuations. The desire to restore the cartel-like conditions on a grand scale goes hand in hand with the benefits enjoyed by structural debtors when exchange rate risk is removed, and the cost of capital is reduced. This is obtained by substituting a single currency for the several national ones that existed previously. And further cost of funds reductions can be obtained by the elimination of inflation premiums, which implies that a the new shared currency is managed according to a strictly conservative monetary policy.

A Mercantilist Bargain

Of course, one might have thought about having all the countries concerned adopt a strong currency that was already existent, namely, the Deutsche mark. But it would have been hard for policy makers in other countries to accept the loss of monetary autonomy in favor of one of their competitors. They would have been accused of selling out the national interest in favor of "annexation" by Germany, and any hint of such an accusation would have been politically explosive.

So they chose to create a duplicate of the mark, the euro, to be managed, according to statute, the same way the original one was. This was also a condition imposed by Germany in order to secure their consent to do away with the symbol of its post-War success and the key element in its export model. All other countries were supposed to benefit in that they immediately acquired a strong currency, without having to secure voters' consent to years of monetary tightening, which would have been necessary to convince markets that they were resolute and credible in their new belief in a seriously anti-inflationary policy. Germany served as a guarantee for the new euro project, from the outset, based on its reputation for monetary stability. From this point of view, it was a boon for structural debtors like Italy, Spain, Ireland, France, and of course Greece. The interest rates for borrowing in these countries fell abruptly.

But what did Germany have to gain? She was lending her reputation, hard won through years of conservative policies, to all these other countries. She would have to be repaid for that, one way or another. She won through the way in which the exchange rates were defined upon each country's entry into the euro, which essentially equated to a substantial under valuation of the mark relative to other currencies. In other words, the definition of parity, at the creation of the euro, allowed Germany to enjoy a real "competitive devaluation" in fact, giving it a strong advantage in exporting to other countries in the zone. What's more, she was spared the competitive devaluations of other European countries (especially Italy), which had periodically threatened her own exports and boosted her imports. This was the price for Germany's consenting to doing away with the mark, and it further strengthened the German model of an export economy.

It was also the beginning of recurring trade-balance difficulties for France, Italy and the others vis-à-vis Germany,[22] especially given that inflation rates did not converge, but on the contrary, prices in almost every country other than Germany continued to go up faster than prices in Germany, further increasing the Federal Republic's competitive advantage.

And so the agreement was sealed in an exchange that was supposed to be balanced: Germany brought its strong currency and lent its conservative and orthodox reputation, while the other countries brought to Germany the advantage of market opportunities, an advantage which they pretended to believe would gradually be reduced in the future as inflation rates converged. As for the industrialists and bankers, they saw in it a way to restore their cartels across a vast single market, a market far greater than they used to enjoy in their domestic economies.

But let's not forget the states and their interest, as organizations, in securing their own survival and access to resources. States too are structural debtors. As such they are particularly sensitive to lending rates. The 1980s and 1990s had brought them their share of problems. When the economies were opened up internationally, this sig-

---

22 Two thirds of European Union countries' foreign trade is with other EU countries.

nificantly reduced their financial capacity — partly because the mobility of goods and of factors of production
made it difficult and costly to tax goods, labor and capital
(which is especially mobile). And partly due to the loss
of the dominant debtor's position they had enjoyed in
their domestic capital markets. In France for instance, the
Treasury was once the largest issuer of bonds, and it had
the power to compel institutional investors to buy these
debt instruments. This allowed it to practice "financial
repression" by maintaining low interest rates for these investors and more generally for the public, and especially
bank depositors through a prohibition of interest payments on demand deposits.[23]

On global financial markets that are much larger and
are beyond the control of individual states, finance min-
istries no longer have much power; it is becoming harder
and harder to increase taxes, while state funding needs
continue to grow, partly because of demographic changes
that are bringing the wave of post-War baby-boomers to
the threshold of retirement.

European states therefore aspire, just like the corporations, to forge a stronger position for borrowers in the

---

23 See Jean-Jacques Rosa and Michel Dietsch, *La répression finan-
cière*, Bonnel, 1981.

financial markets, and they would like to organize a European cartel for that, too. The best indicator is their stub-
bornness in denouncing the "excessive" fiscal competition
by which some of them try to reduce overall tax rates to
attract capital and investors. They would much prefer to
organize a fiscal cartel that would enable them to raise tax
rates all across Europe. Similarly, a single currency should
enable them to more easily restore, among themselves as
among the bankers and other businesses, a cartel of borrowers that would reduce bond rates by the means of the
high price of the currency.

But such a debtors' cartel, like any cartel, can only
function if it limits the amount of the product put on the
market. In this case the product is debt securities issued
by national treasuries: government bonds. Too large a
bond issuance would make the price drop, as investors
would say they already have too much in their portfolios.
And when bond prices go down, it means that issuers
have to offer higher interest rates on these instruments.
That would hardly help in managing the affairs of the various states and would mean the end of their cartel.

For this reason the creation of the single currency had
to be accompanied by an agreement on quotas regarding the issuance of "sovereign" debt, state bonds, issued
in the foreign financial market, so as to avoid flooding

these markets and increasing the governments' cost of funds. Each state, however, like any member of a cartel, has an incentive to cheat and exceed its production quota for debt, and an even stronger incentive when the price set by the cartel is high. Indeed, any debtor that offers a yield even slightly higher than the cartel is likely to issue far more debt than its quota allows. But if they all do the same thing, then they will have to up their payment to lenders, that is the interest rates they offer. The cost of borrowed capital will go up and the cartel of borrowers will lose their rents.

When the price of sovereign bonds is lower, the cost of borrowing capital is higher; so that from the perspective of the member states of the cartel, it is important to avoid letting the price of the bond issues go down. And too much debt leads to greater efforts to monetize the debt, which triggers more inflation following the creation of more currency, which in turn degrades the future value of the currency, which then reduces international demand for euro-denominated bonds. The rule of thumb, therefore, has been to avoid inflation and keep a lid on bond issues. This is precisely the rule of any cartel: a high price, made possible by respecting production quotas. Here, it means a high price for the euro, made possible by "production quotas" on bonds.

But how should the quotas be set for issuing bonds? By imposing a simple rule: Each state has to limit its budget deficit to a fixed ratio of its national product. It is an egalitarian rule that uniformly sets debt emission quotas in proportion to each one's economic size. This is the "Stability Pact", which is the expression of an agreement among a cartel of debtors. It was one of the requirements of the German government, which wanted to ensure that overly lax policies on budget deficits would not ultimately impair the value of the euro, as the successor to the mark. It further enhanced the system by prohibiting the ECB, by statute, from refinancing governments by buying their bonds, and by introducing the so-called "no bailout" clause: A government that took on too much debt would not be financially supported by its more prudent neighbors; in other words, intergovernmental transfers within the zone were forbidden.

However, like all cartel agreements, the one underlying the foundation of the euro was fragile and vulnerable to cheating — as the results have amply demonstrated — and it was soon fractured, then shattered.

The conclusion to be drawn is that a strong single currency is an awesome "borrowing machine." And despite all the precautions of the cartel agreement, that is how it worked. Since the cost of borrowing was significantly lowered, structural debtors borrowed more, and they did so on a massive scale. As it became increasing difficult to collect taxes, states went into debt to compensate; and bankers borrowed heavily to develop their new profession of "hedge fund managers". Their traditional occupation, collecting their liquid deposits and using them to make loans, had indeed been seriously undermined by the global expansion of the financial markets in the 1980s and 90s. Large companies were getting credit directly on the financial markets by issuing bonds instead of using the services of their banks — to the point that one often heard, in those days, references to the "death of the banks." But thanks to the development of new financial techniques, the bankers were able to reinvent their business, by going out in the bond markets as borrowers, too, investing on their own account, with countless sophisticated assets, and entailing considerable risk. They were willing to see their debt increase without significantly increasing their capital, for the time being, in order to "leverage" their positions and significantly increase their profitability. But they also increased their risk.

Of course, these "new bankers" were anxious to minimize the cost of international borrowing, and so for them, as for the states, a currency that was strong and big, in the sense that it was used by several economies, gave them safeguards and at the same time the anti-inflationary benefits of liquidity — which worked together to reduce lending rates.

So these are the structural debtors — states, banks, big corporations — whose previous revenue sources, that were based on market power, have been lost due to the development of globalization and global competition. They have sought by any means to reduce the cost of financing. And the best way was to introduce a strong single currency.[24]

In sum, it is not the goal of reducing transaction costs (which the Commission itself recognized were small, if not negligible) that explains the creation of the euro. And neither is it building of international trade. Economists have wrongly emphasized this aspect because in economics, more trade means more prosperity (and can therefore serve as justification for the euro), and because that field

---

24 Proponents of collusion and cartels at both ends of the political spectrum use to denounce the "ultra-competitiveness" or "ultra-liberalism" of the European economy, both with regard to banks (which now come under the authority of the ECB that represents their collective professional interests, as all central banks do) and to states (which are dead set on removing any "fiscal competition", that is to say, that hope to raise their taxes in concert). This is a complete misdiagnosis: the current European centralizing policies, and the single currency in the first place, are not ultra-liberal at all but constitute essentially a dirigiste, corporatist and statist enterprise.

is familiar to them. But the additional expected growth to be obtained through monetary unification is insignificant in the present circumstance, given that national markets have already been opened wide by globalization.[25] [26]

Nor is increased competition the reason. On the contrary, it is precisely those companies that are cartelized who benefit from the euro — through the price collusion that is facilitated by the single currency.

And it's not a balanced budget or economic growth, either. The Maastricht Treaty did not improve the fiscal balances nor the macroeconomic performance of member states. Rather, it had a negative impact, according to a recent study that backs up the findings of much previous work.[27]

25 Helge Berger and Volker Nitsch, "Zooming Out: The Trade Effect of the Euro in Historical Perspective", Working paper, Free University, Berlin, July 6, 2006.

26 Volker Nitsch added, in July 2008 ("Monetary Integration and Trade : What Do We Know ?") : "In sum, I find little conclusive evidence that the introduction of the euro has measurably affected patterns of trade in Europe. In view of the above reasoning that trade effects can be expected to be particularly strong in Europe, this finding is not particularly encouraging concerning potential trade effects of regional monetary integration."

27 Thushyanthan Baskaran: "Did the Maastricht treaty matter for macroeconomic performance? A difference-in-difference investigation." Kyklos, August 2009.

No, the reason for the euro is that it suits the interests of the structural debtors: states, banks, and big business. Financial considerations and financial benefits are the primary reasons that underpin the creation of their cartel.

Adverse Effects and Self-Destruction

The introduction of this financial cartel has had significant and serious consequences that have belied the promises made by its promoters.

Once in place, the "borrowing machine" has been running at full capacity, due to the behavior of certain states like Greece as much as the behavior of the major banks in Ireland, Germany and France. This hyperactivity has led to a de facto dismantling of the cartel quotas and has forced the ECB to monetize some portion of the debts of states whose solvency is in doubt, while governments have been forced to violate the "no bailout" clause to temporarily save other governments and big banks that took on too much risk.

First of all, easy borrowing has removed the budget constraints that normally curb government spending. While tax revenues stagnated in the 1990s as a proportion of national product, government expenditures have risen continuously without being hindered by the increasing debt burden, first through the period when the economy was steadily expanding, then on a much larger scale during the 2007–2009 crisis.[28]

The Stability Pact could not keep the brakes on for long under the pressure of the crisis, in economies that had no way of implementing an appropriate monetary policy.

This same easy access to financing spared governments from having to struggle with "structural" reforms and from trying to increase competitiveness. Instead of imposing more economic liberalization, the euro has supported the status quo and encouraged true reform paralysis.

But of course the underlying reason for adopting the euro — low-cost borrowing — and the likely consequences on the economy, were hard to "sell" to the public.

Hence the plethora of absurd justifications and dubious claims about the alleged, but unlikely, virtues of the euro. Everything was false in the official argument. And you could see that already in the Treaty of 1992, if you had eyes to see.

28The lack of this kind of balance-sheet constraint, known as a "soft budget constraint", led to the bankruptcy of many Russian entreprises right after the dissolution of the USSR.

3. How All This Will End

"Badly", is the easy answer. Badly, for the euro that is; but nicely, no doubt, for the economies of the member states.

We can make that prognosis based on the well-known instability of cartels that results from the intense incentive to cheat that they generate among their members.

This applies just as well to monetary cartels, especially for currency unions that have been built without a central government having been established beforehand.[29] In a cartel of goods and services, in fact, once an agree-

29 Michael D. Bordo and Lars Jonung, "The Future of the EMU: What Does the History of Monetary Unions Tell Us?", NBER Working Paper N° 7365, September 1999.

ment is reached between the participants as to the quotas of each one, and once the price has gone up, it is in each producer's interest to cheat by slightly lowering its own price, which enables it to sell far more than its quota and to pocket the profits thus obtained, as discussed above. In these circumstances, of course, the quantities supplied to the market increase and the cartel price plummets back toward the level of price competition, which ultimately eliminates the super profit. The cartel then dissolves into a competitive situation. Thus cartels usually last only if there is an institution capable of monitoring the members and enforcing the agreement on prices and quotas. A central government is best placed to fulfill this mission of policing prices and quantities. But absent a government, the cartel inevitably tends to dissolve. In a cartel of debt issuers (whether money or bonds), the problem is the inverse: the objective is to avoid a devaluation of the currency or bonds, which would increase the cost of obtaining financial resources or the cost of money. But the reasoning remains the same, and in this case too the existence of a cartel police is crucial to its survival. This explains how monetary unions can fall apart even when such a central government has been in place, when the latter starts to unravel.[30]

In the case of the euro, we can readily understand the calls for the formation of a federal state that would fulfill this essential supervisory function. In fact, its absence was mitigated by the establishment of the European Central Bank (ECB), which plays exactly that role as to the creation of money. It refrains in principle from buying the debt of member states, which would lead to the creation of massive amounts of Euros that would create inflation and depreciate the currency.

But the same cannot be said for bonds, despite the stability pact that was supposed to limit their "production"; there is no institutional apparatus offering the kind of control that the ECB wields over currency. Under these conditions, the only variable that national governments still can control in order to conduct stabilization policies is the deficit, and so it becomes inevitable to take on enormous debt in times of crisis. But if we go too far in that direction, we end up with worse problems, adding a crisis of insolvency to the initial recession.

---

30 Volker Nitsch, "Have a Break, Have a ... National Currency: When Do Monetary Unions Fall Apart?", CESifo Working Paper N° 1113, January 2004; Andrew K. Rose, "Checking Out: Exits from Currency Unions", Draft, December 15, 2006.

The only solution for widely disparate economies, when there is no way to establish a vast federal budget covering them all and serving as a major shock absorber, is to leave the single currency and return to a national monetary and fiscal policy, one that is "customized" to the specific situation of each national economy. But how can we effect such an exit, and especially, how can we minimize the cost?

The disintegration of a cartel having multiple players could follow too many scenarios to allow us to describe what would happen in advance. The best we can do is to look at a given country and try to ascertain what specific approach to exiting the agreement would be most advantageous.

The idea of getting out is simply not considered by supporters of the euro,[31] who wave the specter of an inevitable economic Apocalypse. By their reckoning, countries returning to a flexible exchange rate would instantaneously lose the confidence of international investors as to the future value of their currency.[32] A massive depreciation would first increase the size — in terms of the

---

31 Barry Eichengreen, "The euro: love it or leave it?" Voxeu.org, 19 November 2007.

32 This was already predicted in Great Britain when it exited the European Monetary System in 1992-93. But nothing of the kind occurred. To the contrary, the British economy profited largely by returning to flexible exchange rates.

---

new national currency, the franc, for example — of the euro-denominated debt (assuming that the euro is still in use, and is still strong). A devaluation of 20% for example, would increase the size of the euro-denominated debt by 20% in francs and as a share of French GDP. Now, it is very unlikely that the French national income would grow by 20% instantaneously upon leaving the euro zone, despite the increased competitiveness that such a depreciation would bring. The burden of <u>net foreign debt</u> as a percentage of French GDP would increase accordingly, only making it more necessary to impose a policy of severe deflation, and we learned in the 1930s how harmful that is.

This vision of an economic Apocalypse following any exit from the single currency is, however, just a last line of defense intended to block any challenge to the euro. Europhiles have exhausted their previous arguments, which were each radically disproven by experience.[33] But this last line of defense is just as unrealistic as the previous ones.

On the one hand, the growth of public debt in the event of exiting the euro, followed by a devaluation of the new currency, is overestimated in this reckoning. And, on the other hand, a major devaluation of the euro, <u>prior to</u>

---

33 See "Les promesses de l'euro, tout était faux", at the author's site, http://jeanjacques.rosa.pagesperso-orange.fr

the exit, would solve the problem completely. Then exiting the euro would produce only net benefits for the
country in question.

A More Realistic Assessment of the Cost of Exit

Let's accept first that in the worst case (which does
not apply to France), an insolvent state will default on
its foreign debt, as Argentina for example did, a few years
ago, and as Greece could soon be forced to do.

Increased foreign debt is thus no longer important, as
it will not be repaid regardless of the amount. At the same
time, devaluation brings the currency down to a level that
restores the international price competitiveness of the
economy which has a chance then to return to growth.
This is what happened in Argentina after an intense but
brief period of crisis.

Apart from this extreme case, one must keep in mind
the order of magnitude of debt that can be increased by
devaluation upon exiting a system of fixed exchange rates
or a shared currency:

Take the example of a country with a debt of 80% of
its GDP, which is not far from the case of France. Of this
80%, foreign debt might represent 2/3 or just less than

53% of GDP.[34] Returning to the franc might be accompanied, as a middle-of-the-road assumption, by a 20% devaluation against the euro (if it still exists). In France, foreign debt would be increased from 53% to just under 64% of GDP, which is hardly an economic "cataclysm".

Total public debt, domestic and foreign, actually goes up due to the increase of the foreign component: In our hypothetical case it goes from 80% of GDP to 91% of GDP when the foreign component rose from 53% to 64% of GDP, as explained above. Remember also that several countries, including Italy and Belgium, have lived for many years with public debt substantially exceeding 100% of GDP, especially in the case of Italy, because the debt is largely domestic and not foreign. A devaluation of a new lira would not increase it.

When it comes to domestic debt in Euros (owned by residents), we will assume that they are instantly transformed into francs for the same amount. The exit from the euro should in fact convert one euro to one franc, for simplicity's sake. Holders of domestic debt in the amount of € 100 would find themselves owners of 100 francs in debt.

---

34 Here, we assume that the total foreign debt is also the net debt. But if the State also has foreign receivables, the total net debt may be less, which makes difference since foreign receivables will also be increased (in francs, assuming the exit from the euro is followed by devaluation). But let's stick with the hypothesis of a net foreign debt of 80% of GDP.

This would not affect their standard of living. Their salaries would go from 100 Euros (for example) to 100 francs and the GDP of X Euros would be converted to the same X francs. There is no increase in the debt burden.

At the same time, doing this would have major positive effects: It would restore international competitiveness, not only vis-à-vis third countries (the United States and countries that have a fixed exchange rate against the dollar) but also potentially (as explained below) vis-à-vis the present member countries of the euro zone, Germany in particular.

This would open up real prospects for a return to sustained growth in a country where exports account for about one third of the total activity. International competitiveness is therefore a critical source of growth for both exporters and for industries whose products compete with imports.

The result of the exit from the euro, followed by devaluation, would prove to be positive, because the capacity to service the debt depends primarily on a return to economic growth (which lowers the debt/GDP ratio).

<u>There is a better way, however, and that is to do it the other way around, by devaluing the euro first and then getting out; then there will be no need to devalue the new national currency against the euro.</u>

The Franc Might Be Devalued Only Slightly — Or Not At All

The strategy of devaluing the euro before seceding from the monetary union allows us to avoid any "Apocalypse" at all during the transition to a national currency. It consists of taking advantage of developments already under way for the benefit of the country.

If the euro were taken down to its initial level, or just about at parity with the dollar or even below it, that would restore the competitiveness of economies in the region vis-à-vis the U.S. economy and the economies whose currencies are linked to the dollar (China, for example, and other Asian countries). Even supporters of the euro acknowledge that, although they have previously argued strenuously to the contrary.

Continuing down this path until one euro equals one dollar, or, preferably, one euro equals 0.84 dollar, as was the case shortly after its launch in 2000, under the authority of Mr. Duisenberg, the decline would lead the single currency to a level close to theoretical equilibrium.

Under such conditions, France for instance (but this would also apply to countries of the "periphery" of the euro zone) would still suffer from an exchange rate handicap, but only within the euro area, that is to say essentially vis-à-vis Germany.

A quick calculation shows that the difference in France's labor costs accumulated since 1999 with regard to Germany is about 12%, or say, maybe, 15% to round it up. France is at a disadvantage to Germany still, despite the decline of the euro, as Germany benefits from it just as much as France does.

If we assume that France can regain competitiveness compared to the rest of the world via a less drastic variant, by aiming at a rate of one euro to the dollar, France would still need an additional 15% exchange rate haircut to restore its competitiveness against the mark (or the "euro-mark", if that's what is left), especially since the mark would appreciate during this transition. This condition could be met at a rate of 0.85 dollars per euro, that is to say the exchange rate that prevailed in 2000.

At this price, no further devaluation would be required upon exiting the union. There would be no increase in foreign debt or massive outflows of capital in anticipation of a future depreciation. And this "pre-devaluation" of the euro, we should note, would help Germany as much as France. The euro exit could be accomplished calmly and without any sign of the catastrophe forecast by the pundits.

Conditions for Success of the "Devaluation-then-Secession" Approach

The decision must be made immediately after the target euro–dollar parity rate is reached. We will need to study the point more closely to see what that desirable level of parity is, and of course that optimal parity point must remain confidential. In consideration of likely U.S. reactions, in particular, it may be more acceptable to plan for just a slight depreciation of the euro before acting, together with a moderate devaluation of the new franc following. There might be quite a variety of combinations of euro depreciations before the exit and franc depreciations after the exit that would work. This must be studied and tested, as should be the necessary dialogue with other countries. But the basic principle remains.

In any case, while we are waiting (and the waiting period has better be short, as the need for economic recovery is urgent), we must support and encourage the decline of the euro, for example by putting pressure on the ECB to monetize the debt of member states as it does now,[35] and

35 This was written in early 2011 for the French edition of the book. Since then, Mr. Draghi has replaced Mr. Trichet as head of the ECB, the scope of the program of buying back southern governments' bonds has been increased, and the euro has been depreciating slightly vis-à-vis the dollar, from about $1.40 at the beginning of 2011 fall quarter to about $1.27 or 1.26 by mid-January 2012. This is a move corre-

disseminating any information that would lead the markets to anticipate a shift to a weaker euro, and in particular letting it be known that we intend to make our exit.

THE URGENCY

There is another reason not to waste time. The greatest risk would be that the southern countries exit the euro before we do. If that happens, the value of a "northern" residual euro would go up against the dollar, and France's exit would be much more painful. There is indeed a potential competition for exit. We would remain caught in the same trap we are in now, but worse in that the euro area would comprise only those members that are structurally most suited to a conservative monetary policy, and thus further from the optimum for France.

Under those conditions, with a euro that would re-evaluate, we would have to accept a serious depreciation of the new franc when we exited, with a corresponding increase in net foreign debt. That would really hurt our economy.

In other words, the next time there is a substantial depreciation of the euro, it is advisable to act quickly and boldly, because the more pronounced the depreciation,

sponding to the policy I advocate, but much remains to be done to reach $1.00 or less. Then watch for the exit.

the more the drawbacks of secession will be reduced.[36] And history rarely offers a second chance.

But, of course, taking into account our analysis of the vested interests as presented earlier, making any change on such a large scale threatens the political equilibrium at the most profound level.

THE POLITICAL CONSEQUENCES

A radical policy shift will inevitably affect the credibility of many leaders who have actively supported the creation of the euro and European centralization more broadly. But such reversals are not unknown in politics and a government that manages to pull off such a transition will receive an enormous return for the risk taken. Voters will be elated with the return to economic growth that results. Politics, after all, is the art of making possible that which is necessary.

---

36 It has to be done all at once, preferably with banknotes prepared in advance. But we can also allow some time for the manual exchange of banknotes, since most of money is actually not in cash.

In practical terms, it would be sufficient to decree the instantaneous conversion of 100 euros 100 francs for all bank deposits. These transactions could be performed without major capital outflows, if the prior devaluation of the euro has been great enough. Then holders of exported euros would not have much to gain from any anticipated subsequent devaluation.

All that being said, it is neither the electoral conse-quences nor the tactical process that matters most. The greatest political consequence of seceding from the euro is that we could reverse the trend away from democracy that we have had to deal with in recent decades.

The drive toward European unification, of which the single currency is the most salient sign, has actually sent us backwards in terms of democratic processes. What a paradox in the era of democracy's triumph around the world! It is easy to understand how the regression works. There has been a dilution of the influence of national elec-torates, and a strengthening of the autonomy of the ex-ecutive branches at the national and supranational levels. At the same time, lobbying groups have more power and so do unelected supervisory authorities, such as the Euro-pean Central Bank.

The dilution of the voter's power relates to parliamen-tary elections, on the one hand, and control of executive decisions, on the other.

According to the Constitution, the French electorate has 100% choice of their representatives. By contrast, in the European system, the French electorate as a whole can only hope to designate representatives in the Continental Parliament in proportion to their population compared to the entire EU. According to the rules, that is about 60 million people out of 450 million Europeans. That means about 13% of the parliamentarians in Strasbourg. The French citizen's vote is being diluted by something more than a factor of 7.

When it comes to appointing the executive (the government in France and the Council of Ministers in the European Treaty), we see that 100% of the members of government are appointed by the elected representatives of the citizens (President of the Republic, and the Parliament) in the Constitution, whereas in the European Treaty we have one minister out of 25, or 4% of the European Council. Here, the power of the voter is diluted by a factor of 25.

Moreover, centralized policies adopted over a broader and necessarily more heterogeneous area are less likely to reflect the preferences of French voters.

It follows that the transition to continental policy making can only reduce the democratic satisfaction of the national electorates if they have specific preferences and do not constitute together a "single people" with the same preferences as those of other countries. It is this fundamental question that gives real substance to the debate on whether or not there is such a thing as a "European people". This is not an ideological or speculative matter. Are political preferences distributed similarly ("homothetic") or are they dissimilar across the various "national peoples" of member countries? Heterogeneity of preferences means that a centralized system cannot deliver democratic results efficiently.

But on top of these two problems, if they aren't bad enough, there is a third one. Shifting to a larger base of operations means a dilution of democracy and a dramatic strengthening of lobbying groups and political and administrative personnel.

Indeed, centralization, which in this case corresponds to an increase in the size of the polity (the EU becoming the space of reference), entails a considerable gain of power and resources for the political and administrative class as a whole (which we may refer to as the "executive class"[37]) and for pressure groups.

We know[38] that regulations are equivalent to taxes accompanied by subsidies. They effectively impose ad-

---

37 We can treat all government officials and politicians as one group, or a single entity, to the extent that these professionals share a common interest (when it comes to regulation, for instance) and all the more so as there is fusion of careers, rather than a differentiation between those who monitor and those who are monitored, as I showed in my article "Officials, Policy and Democracy" published in *Le Figaro* on November 28, 1997.

38 from an analysis by Nobel laureate George Stigler, "The theory of economic regulation" and see also Richard A. Posner, "Taxation by Regulation", both in *The Bell Journal of Economics and Management*, Spring 1971.

ditional costs on certain categories of stakeholders and provide benefits or transfers to other categories. Thus a policy of supporting farm prices (above current market prices) means a levy on income for consumers of these products, and at the same time a subsidy to growers. It is a tax together with a transfer.

Now, taking regulations that affect a nation of 50, 60 or 70 million people and applying them to 450 million people obviously changes the balance sheet corresponding to these quasi taxes and transfers. A rule that represents a 6-euro tax and transfer in the first case would come to 45 euros within the Europe-wide framework.

The power of the executive who decides on such transactions is increased by the same extent — by 1 to 13 — because he can apply these same rules to a much larger client base. Career rewards in the executive branch become greater in proportion to their increased power. Just as career prospects are greater in the largest firms when they increase their sales, as larger firms generally pay more than smaller ones do, the prestige and salaries of bureaucrats and policy makers are related to the large size of the entity which they govern.

But this is not the only transformation caused by centralization. All the various lobbies benefit just as much. Instead of having to negotiate with 15 or 25 independent national authorities, they can focus on one principal authority and gain access to the whole market of 450 million consumers. The chance to secure desirable policies ("rent-seeking")[39] across the board is well worth any greater investment that may be needed to secure those policies.

This means that at first glance the cost of lobbying in Europe is divided by 25 (or more recently 27) because of regulatory centralization, compared to what it was before centralization.

So it is no surprise that lobbying is such a big business in Brussels. It is also no surprise that regulations are proliferating in this large ensemble, since the benefits they now offer, to those who provide them as well as to those who seek them, have increased considerably. The amount of lobbying aimed at any federal supervisory authority can be greatly amplified compared to what was directed at each national authority. Some 10 or 15 national lobbying budgets or more have been dropped, freeing up resources; and also the results of successful lobbying are multiplied by 15, 20 or 25 due to centralization.

In addition, the large size encourages more lobbies to be formed. In a small country, there are not always enough

---

39 This is the phenomenon of "rent-seeking" studied by Gordon Tullock.

producers of a certain product to create an effective interest group.[40]

But in a large country, the critical threshold has usually already been reached. There are enough producers to
create a lobby. And many more lobbies will be created
when the market is larger.

In sum, centralization, first and foremost through the
use of a single currency, has made society less democratic.
The shift to the continental forum has concealed a continued and retrograde use of bureaucratic centralism, a constant reinforcement of the executive and of cartels that
shuts the public out of the political game and takes us
away from democratic practices by effectively removing
any substantial macroeconomic, financial, or regulatory
question from the public debate.

By reversing the trend in the monetary arena, by exiting the euro, we can restore the conditions for an open
discussion of these policies. Such a change will revital-
ize political debates by giving them meaningful content
again, breaking the left–right and public–private collusion that currently reduce national disputes to personal
confrontations between individual figures who have no
interest in ordinary people and their future.

---

40 Mancur Olson shows in particular how hard it can be to create such an interest group.

Secession, of course, can only be truly considered if it receives broad public support across a wide range of opinions. It is only realistic, in other words, if it supports or even restores democracy, which is the foundation of our republican constitution. Getting the franc out of the euro, and returning to monetary independence, is a first step in restoring our democracy which has been continually eroded, undermined and over-run by the persistent and collusive drive of the unionists since the 1980s.

CONCLUSION

The War of Secession has begun. It is not just between states, but between people concerned about their standard of living, on the one hand, and national treasuries, banks, and big business, on the other, who intend to defend to the bitter end both their advantage as borrowers and their intra-European cartels. This war will not stop until the dissolution of the euro, which should have positive effects on the economies of the zone in its present configuration. The defeasance of the toxic asset that is the euro will improve the standard of living.

Coming after a period of necessary depreciation of the euro, it would cost us little or nothing to get out of it. France would regain competitiveness both in respect to Germany and the rest of the world. We would no longer need to raise taxes, deflation would be avoided, and economic growth would take off. Today, beneficiaries of the euro are found among high officials and big companies that are not exporting much but are entrenched abroad, where their profits do not depend much on the health of the domestic market. It is this fraction of opinion, an influential minority, that has to be brought to accept the demise of the euro, or rather the return to the franc. A government that could plainly state the economic evidence, and that would have enough conviction to translate it into reality, would earn the gratitude of the vast majority of the population for the growth that would follow an exit from the monetary union. Just remember the success that came with recognizing economic reality and the freeing of competitive energy that the Gaullist government brought in 1958.

That would certainly require a 180-degree reversal of official speeches and current policies, rooted in more than a quarter century of rhetoric. But such reversals are not unprecedented. Thus in the early 1980s the Socialists, against all economic reason, initiated a program of nationalization, which led (along with other factors) to macroeconomic disaster, but suited the ideology of the electorate, an ideology that had been constantly pounded into them since 1945. Once it was proven that this policy was a failure and it could not be sustained, the socialist government was able to launch a complete reversal and actually began privatizing, after an intermediate stage that was basically a "neither, nor" policy.

In the short term, however, it appears unlikely that Germany and France can take this kind of initiative. The elections are now, and the positive effects of a new monetary policy usually require a year or more to take effect. Timing is everything. And also it would probably be inappropriate to embark on a difficult public debate before the elections. But the amounts of sovereign debt that mature in 2012, 2013 and 2014 make it clear that the issue will come up again, and even more acutely, in the coming years. This will be at the forefront of the public debate when the time comes, especially since we have no reason to expect any spectacular economic recovery in the interim.

We are left with a difficult question: what to do with the ECB? We know that international institutions, like states, rarely die, and the interest group represented by the bank in Frankfurt is no insignificant player. Its ability to survive is probably high. One might therefore allow it to stay in place, as some people suggest, to manage an "optional" common currency, one that has to compete freely with national currencies and is based on a basket of currencies — as was at one time considered for the ECU.

This new, competitive euro could then be chosen as the unit of accounting for any businesses that would prefer it to national currencies. As such it must be understood that the new euro would be most useful as a management tool for European cartels, which are such a handicap for our economies. But if that is the price we must pay to gain some room for maneuver for national monetary policies, why not? ... with reservations, however, and after further reflection.

The key is to act decisively at the right time and seize the opportunity presented by the devaluation of the euro to get out of the single-currency quagmire at the lowest cost, by adopting a strategy exactly the opposite of ever-increasing federalism; that is, a policy of returning to monetary independence and the real competition of international prices. The laboratory of real-life experience has confirmed the conclusions of economic theory, and doubt can no longer be entertained.

Paradoxically, the euro has been a reactionary and undemocratic parenthetical digression in an era of organizational decentralization and increased competition. It is now necessary and imperative to drop it, to return to monetary independence, and to recreate the franc: a franc that was wrongly vilified, a franc that might have to be depreciated, but a franc that at last would be free.

Appendix I. The French Banking Cartel

According to *Le Monde*, September 21, 2010,

The Competition Authority has made public Monday, September 20, its decision to impose sanctions on eleven major French banks, amounting to 384.9 million Euros, for having set, "in concert", interchange fees on check processing that were not justified between 2002 and 2007.

...The fine imposed on banks set a record in this arena, which was already convicted in 2000 for an anti-competition agreement on real estate loans (174.5 million Euros). This is the third largest penalty handed out by the Competition Authority, after the fines on mobile phone operators in 2005 (534 million) and the steel-trading cartel in 2008 (575.4 million)....

In addition, the Competition Authority is particularly hard on those banks that are "repeat offenders" that were convicted in 2000, Crédit Mutuel, Caisses d'Épargnes (now BPCE), Société Générale, Crédit Agricole, Crédit Lyonnais (LCL) and BNP Paribas. The fine for those six institutions has been increased by 20%.

The Authority also notes that five institutions played an active role in establishing these wrongful commissions to the detriment of traders: Crédit Agricole, Crédit Mutuel, La Poste, Caisses d'Épargne and BNP Paribas....

"The sanctioned behaviors are highly illustrative of how the banking world functions; it is not helping its clients take advantage of a general reform of interest rates that would provide greater economic efficiency," says a source within the Authority.

And further: "There is always a consensus in this sector not to change anything, to keep the overall equilibrium in place. This is hardly what we mean by competition!"

APPENDIX II. "THE EURO, AN OPPORTUNITY FOR FRANCE, AN OPPORTUNITY FOR EUROPE"

Or, the alleged virtues of the euro seen by political, business and academic elites before the euro was adopted. Excerpts from an article published in *Le Monde*, 28 October 1997:

> The EU member states and many companies
> have already started preparing for the introduction
> of the euro. This is not an end in itself. It will bring
> together European citizens, providing them more
> welfare, cohesion and capacity for action.
>
> Do we fully appreciate the enormity of this
> event? Have we taken stock of the challenges and
> opportunities arising from the implementation of
> the Economic and Monetary Union? Do we know
> that the euro will bring:

1. The logical complement of the single market. Europe has suffered enough from currency fluctuations over the last twenty-five years; it is time to set irrevocable conversion rates on the currencies of its member states. To not do so is to condemn us to the risk of speculative attacks and to pay the price forever, especially in the form of higher interest rates.

2. A common price of reference for all the countries in the euro zone, which will foster competition and stimulate trade. By this means it will ensure attractive prices that the consumer can actually compare; consumers will have better choices as more quality services come on the market.

3. Sound management of public finances. This is necessary anyway. But coordinated at the European level, it will promote growth by providing a large homogeneous market, and will facilitate the moderation of taxes and low interest rates. It will benefit investors, consumers and businesses as well, as the latter will be able to develop research, business and employment.

4. Expanded opportunities for corporate finance and the investment of our savings in a financial market operating on a global scale.

5. A means for simplification and cost reduction in transactions within the Union (as there will be no more exchange rate risk, cross-border payments will cost less....

6. A recognized currency that can compete with the dollar and the yen. The euro will enable Europe, as the world's greatest trading power, to

express its real economic size. The European Central Bank will ensure stability in purchasing power in our daily lives and in our travels abroad. The euro will be a concrete symbol of European identity and will assure the European Union a central position in the international arena.

7. In a Europe unified by its economy and currency, citizens and businesses will now have complete freedom of movement, and can build deeper relationships. A new sense of shared goals can then arise in the social, cultural and political spheres, so that we can forge a more harmonious and democratic Europe.

All these benefits of the euro are still not well known to European populations. Yet the successful adoption of the new currency requires everyone's full confidence, and to get there we need to see strong expressions of enthusiasm. Everyone needs to feel they are part of this. It is high time to raise this awareness and take ownership of the euro at all levels.

...The euro will be a cornerstone of a new sense of unity. It is an act of confidence in the future, a sign of hope and optimism, which will enable Europe to better achieve its destiny and enter fully into a twenty-first century based on peace and freedom.

Signatories:

Michel Albert, a member of the Monetary Policy Council; Edmond Alphandéry, Chairman of EDF; Jacques Attali, a state councilor; Robert Baconnier, CEO of Bureau Francis Lefebvre; René

Barberye, CEO of the Centre National des Caisses d'Epargne et de Prévoyance; Claude Bebear, Chairman AXA-UAP; Jean-Louis Beffa, Chairman of Saint-Gobain; Christian Blanc, former chairman of Air France; Christian de Boissieu, academic; economist and journalist Jean Boissonnat; Philippe Bourguignon, President of Club Med; Monique Bourven, President and CEO State Street Banque SA; Hervé Carré, Director of Monetary Affairs at the European Commission; Jérôme Clément; President of "France 5," a public television network; Bertrand Collomb, Chairman of Lafarge; Paul Coulbois, Professor Emeritus; Lucien Douroux, Managing Director of the Caisse Nationale du Crédit Agricole; Jean-René Fourtou, President of Rhône-Poulenc; Jean-Marie Gorse, National President of the Young Business Leaders (CJD); Gilbert Hyvernant, CEO of the French Red Cross; Jean Kahn, President of the European Advisory Commission on "Racism–Xenophobia"; Philippe Lagayette, General Manager of the Caisse des Dépôts et Consignations; Pascal Lamy, Director General of Crédit Lyonnais; Jacques de Larosière, President of the EBRD; Daniel Lebègue, Vice President of BNP; Robert Leon, Manager of the Executive Board of Suez-Lyonnaise des eaux; Jean Miot, President of the AFP; Thierry de Montbrial, a member of the Institute of France; Etienne Pflimlin, President of Crédit Mutuel; Jean-François Pons, Director General Adjunct of the European Commission; René Ricol, President of the Supreme Council of the Order of Accountants (CSOEC); Jacques Rigaud, President of RTL; Gérard Trémège, President of the Assembly of Chambers of Commerce and Industry.